CHINESE FROGS AND INDIAN DOGS: EATING AND DRINKING AROUND THE WORLD

Tony Mant

MINERVA PRESS

LONDON

MONTREUX LOS ANGELES SYDNEY

**CHINESE FROGS AND INDIAN DOGS: EATING AND
DRINKING AROUND THE WORLD**
Copyright © Tony Mant 1997

ISBN 1 86106 607 4

First Published 1997 by
MINERVA PRESS
195 Knightsbridge,
London SW7 1RE.

Printed in Great Britain for Minerva Press

CHINESE FROGS AND INDIAN DOGS: EATING AND DRINKING AROUND THE WORLD

Contents

Chinese Frogs

I first visited Singapore in 1966 when I was in the RAF and spent a month at the RAF base at Changi. I learned to use chopsticks there and we ate regularly at the roadside stalls in Changi village. The food, cooked to order in huge woks, was delicious and we never experienced any gastric problems.

I had not spent any more time in Singapore until 1985, when I was on a return trip from mainland China. I had passed through the international airport a few years before on the way to Indonesia and, as we landed, got a feeling of déjà vu. It seemed that the main airport now was on the old RAF base at Changi and what had been the civil airport was now the Singapore Air Force base.

There had been many other changes in Singapore and most of the old buildings had been replaced with modern skyscrapers. There was an exhibition on at the time in which my agent was participating with other companies that he represented. We did not have an appointment with Singapore Telecom until the afternoon, so he picked me up in the morning from my hotel and dropped me in the centre of the city, so that I could look around whilst he went to the exhibition. He urged me to leave my heavy briefcase, holding all the material that I needed for our appointment, in his car so that I did not have to carry it on my shopping trip.

This seemed a good idea, but I was to regret it. He had arranged to pick me up where he had dropped me, but did not arrive until an hour after the agreed time. My briefcase also contained my passport, traveller's cheques and return ticket. I became increasingly concerned the later he became, and the experience taught me to never again put all my eggs in one briefcase.

That evening, the head of the agent company had arranged a meal for all the people who were taking part in the exhibition, to which I was also invited. There were about twenty of us and we had a wide selection of dishes, including fresh, warm prawns and a huge plate of frogs' legs. The meal was very good and convivial, with many reminiscences of what had happened to Singapore over the years.

We lingered at the entrance to the restaurant, saying our goodbyes and thanks. In this area were a number of tanks containing live fish which could be selected by diners for their meal. I had experienced this in many parts of the world and always felt a bit squeamish about choosing something to be killed for me to eat.

What I had never seen before was another glass cabinet which was filled with about twenty large, green frogs. It seemed that you could select your frog or frogs and then have their legs for dinner. An acquaintance told me some years later that seeing a Chinese chef preparing a frog to be eaten had turned him into a vegetarian. My hosts took this for granted, but I am sure that the gusto with which I had eaten the frogs' legs would have been less had I noticed the display on the way into the restaurant and not on the way out.

Iranian *Dizi*

I first visited Iran in 1966 whilst I was in the RAF and the Shah was still in power. My colleagues and I agreed that the Iranian women were some of the loveliest in the world. My next visit was nearly thirty years later, after the Islamic Revolution, since when all the lovely ladies, from the age of eight, had been required to wear all-enveloping black cloaks in public. Those I met absolutely hated it, and there were minor signs of rebellion, with many wearing make-up and coloured headscarves. Most of the entertainment is now in people's homes, behind locked doors. There, the lovely ladies emerge from their cloaks like butterflies, with plunging necklines and miniskirts.

The food was much better than I remembered and was remarkably inexpensive. One lunchtime, we went to a *Dizi* restaurant near my agent's office for *Ob Goosht*. *Ob Goosht* means water and meat, that is, a stew. It is called *Dizi* when it is cooked slowly in an oven for many hours.

Dizi restaurants only serve this one dish for a fixed price. Each diner is served with a small earthenware jug and a pestle and mortar. This is accompanied by communal dishes of marinated mixed herbs, salad, raw onion and flat Arabic bread. The bread is torn into small pieces and dropped into the mortar bowl and some herbs are added. Then the liquid in the jug, together with the chick peas in the stew, is poured into the bowl. The mixture is pounded with the pestle and then eaten with the salad and raw onion.

This is done in stages until only the meat is left in the jug, when it too is subjected to the same procedure. The lamb is very tender and delicious. The meal is accompanied with Ayran, which is plain yoghurt mixed with water.

Whilst we were eating, my host pointed out some *Hezzbollahi*. The 'i' on the end of the word indicates 'belonging to' in Farsi. They are identified by being bearded and wearing no neckties. We had met the deputy director of the Iranian Civil Aviation Authority that morning and I was a bit surprised that he had a two day stubble and an open-necked shirt. I was informed that shaving and wearing a tie was an act of rebellion against the fundamentalist regime and was therefore career threatening. I was clean-shaven and had worn a tie on all the visits that we had made, but I was assured that customers got vicarious enjoyment from the 'rebellion' of their visitors.

I had first tasted pistachio nuts on my earlier visit to Iran and told my agent of this when eating some in his home. This is a mistake in such countries, as the host always feels obliged to make a gift of whatever is mentioned. I was presented with two, one-kilo packs of pistachios to bring home. My kids have always thought them disgusting and would not touch them. My wife is not too keen either, so I set to eating my way through them. Some weeks after my return, I broke a nut open and discovered a live, very active maggot inside. I then checked a number of other nuts and found that more than fifty per cent of them contained maggots. By this time I had eaten about half a kilo.

Mathäser Mayhem

On one of my many visits to Munich, I visited the Mathäser Beer Hall, which is huge and is said to be the biggest pub in the world. I ordered a *Mass* (a litre of beer) and some *Radi* (huge, white, thinly sliced radish) and settled down to listen to the oompah band playing on the raised dais in the centre of the hall and to watch the customers. Although it was early, there was a bit of action already.

I watched an argument between two of a group of basically happy people develop to the point at which they stalked off to the Gents toilet to settle it. They came back after twenty minutes, both unmarked, and then reconciled their differences in the 'arms round shoulders, glass clinking, friends forever' way that drunks do.

At the same time, at another table, was a respectable, middle-aged couple and another powerfully built, long-haired and moustachioed man who seemed very bleary of eye. He eventually slumped down on his arms and went to sleep. His companions tried to wake him without success and eventually got up and left, smiling embarrassedly and shrugging their shoulders, not knowing what to do. As they passed my table they told me that they did not like to leave him like that, but that they had to go. He was not a friend of theirs, but had sat down at their table and they had got chatting, as happens in beer halls.

They left and the man slept on. A couple of similarly wild-looking men, who appeared to know the sleeper, saw him in passing and made some effort to wake him. They shook him, lifted his head, and talked loudly to him but he just slumped back down and continued sleeping.

Then one of the muscular serving ladies, who carry six litre *Masses* of beer in each hand (many use trolleys these days but she did not), came to deliver orders and take new ones, and saw the man slumped on one of her tables. She looked pointedly at him, but then ignored him whilst she handed out the beers and took orders. She then went to his table to collect the empty glasses of the couple who had left.

Without a pause in her routine, she lifted his head up by the hair and slapped him vigorously to and fro, half a dozen times across the face. It seemed that the whole beer hall, including the oompah band, went silent and I could feel my mouth gaping in amazement. He shook his head a few times, disbelievingly, and I expected a violent reaction to take place, but he just pulled himself together and wandered off meekly.

Indonesian Pigeon

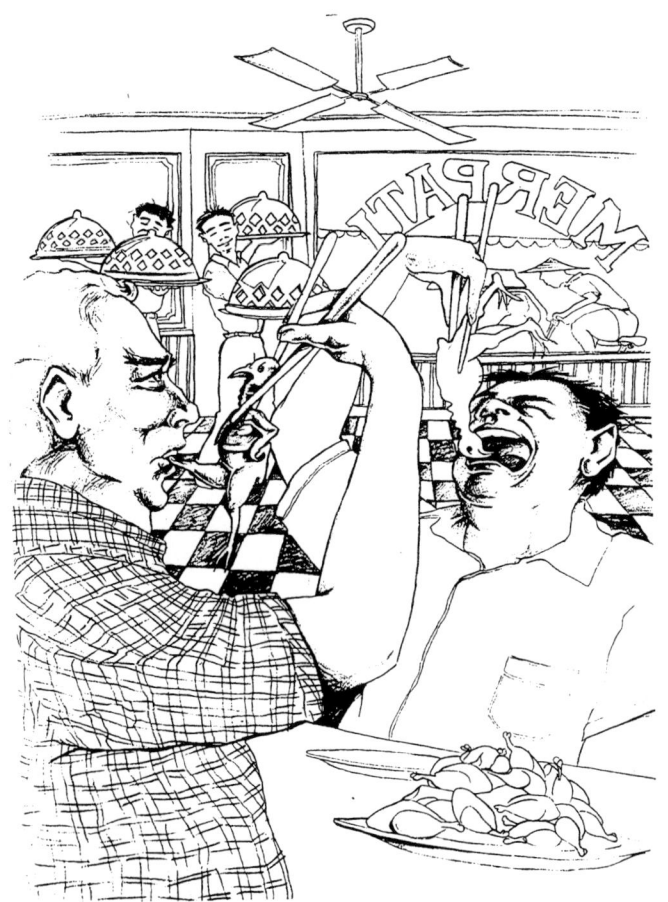

When I was working for a Bavarian electronics company based in Munich, I was responsible, for a time, for selling secure, long range radio communications systems worldwide. The company had formed a liaison with a Swiss encryption equipment company, who had a very high international reputation for their products. The two companies had achieved some success in selling their systems to the Indonesian Ministry of Foreign Affairs (MOFA) for their diplomatic communications between the headquarters in Jakarta and their embassies and consulates around the world.

I made my first visit to Jakarta in the June of 1982 to meet our agent and customer there. Our contact in the agent company was a Chinese Christian, although he had a very Indonesian sounding name – 'Kadri'. In spite of the various actions which had been taken against the Chinese in Indonesia in recent years, Mr Kadri seemed to have a very good relationship with the MOFA. The key person in MOFA was a neighbour of his and their families mixed socially.

Indonesia has a deserved reputation for official corruption, and the MOFA were buying similar equipment from three different manufacturers. This makes no sense logistically, as it is usual to standardise on one manufacturer's equipment for commonality of spares, test equipment, etc. It appeared that equipment was bought from three manufacturers, as this meant that three sets of 'consultancy' fees could be received, rather than one. On a later visit to the Ministry, just before Christmas, the agent opened his briefcase in the customer's office and handed over bundles of notes. I had not been prepared for this and must have shown surprise, as I had never seen such a payment made as openly as this. The customer showed no embarrassment at all. He grinned and said that it was not all for him and that he had to share it around his department.

Mr Kadri took me out to eat in the evenings and on one occasion asked if the English ate pigeons. I replied that they did, and that I liked them. Shortly afterwards, a plate of small, braised pigeon carcasses arrived and I set to with great concentration to eat them with my chopsticks. I had been very careful during the meal to avoid using my left hand whilst eating, as Mr Kadri had said that this was offensive in a mainly Muslim country. He had also said that it really made people recoil, even him who was a Christian, when a foreigner handed something like brochures or letters over with their left hand.

I found gripping the carcass with the chopsticks and trying to tear the tightly bound flesh away with my teeth extremely difficult. When I looked up to see how Mr Kadri was getting along, I saw that his plate was quite empty. I questioned this, and was told that the birds were very young, with soft bones and that everything was eaten, bones and all. I did just that, in order not to lose face, wondering with some trepidation what it would do to my digestion.

It did not seem to cause any problems and I returned to the UK in good shape. On my next visit to Indonesia, we went to the same restaurant and I was laughing with the agent, recalling my surprise when I had realised that I had to eat the birds whole, when a large plate of pigeons arrived in front of me.

Turkish Brain

I have visited Turkey several times over many years and have usually enjoyed the food. My first meal on a visit after many years' break, was a *Mezze* in Ankara. This is a meal consisting of a variety of vegetable and meat dishes from which everyone helps themselves. One of the dishes was sheep's brain, which was presented in its natural form. It looked just like a brain, grey and hemispherical, with many folds and convolutions. I eyed this with some apprehension throughout the meal and finally succumbed to my host's urging to try his favourite dish. It was fairly bland and had the consistency of cold mousse.

This was before the mad cow crisis in 1995/6 which was apparently caused by feeding cows ground up remnants of sheep. The similar brain disease of scrapie, which sheep had suffered from for more than a hundred years, seemed to have transferred to cows. I had been aware of this for some years, which was another source of apprehension about eating sheep's brain. Surprisingly, there still does not seem to have been the same concern that scrapie can transfer to humans in the way that BSE is thought to. I related my Turkish experience to my French teacher, and she said that brain is given extensively to infants in France. It is often mixed with mashed potato and she said that her children had loved it. There must be some Francophobic conclusions that can be drawn from this.

A colleague who was travelling with me had good memories of a fairly simple meal that he had enjoyed on a previous visit. The restaurant took some finding in the furniture-making area near Ankara airport. Turkish drivers do not seem to carry maps of the city, they keep stopping and asking directions. The restaurant was very simple and only served one dish which was lamb, slowly roasted for many hours. This is bought by weight and is served on flat, Arabic type bread. It is eaten with more bread and raw onion and, when the meat is finished, the bread on which the meat is served is consumed. This is delicious with all the juices of the meat soaked into it, but very fatty.

The traditional drink to accompany this is *Ayran* which is plain yoghurt mixed with water. Fingers are used to eat, and there was a large communal washroom at the back of the restaurant for washing hands and faces before and after the meal. We ate about two kilos of meat between four of us and it was the most delicious I have ever tasted. However, at home we have had a low fat diet for many years and I must have consumed more fat than I normally eat in a month. When I awoke after a short rest before dinner, it felt as if the meat, fat and raw onion, together with the *Ayran*, had congealed into one big lump in my stomach. I was sick and immediately felt better, and went on to another large meal that evening in which I managed to eat my share but avoided the fatty dishes and *Ayran*.

Sheep's Legs in Lahore

On my first visit to Pakistan I spent a couple of days in Karachi and then flew on to Lahore. Whilst I was queuing to check in at the airport, a man standing by the check in desk and facing back towards the queue started staring at me. I began to feel uncomfortable, and when I reached him he spoke and said he thought that we had met before. I said that I did not think so as this was my first visit to Pakistan. He then said that he used to work for Singapore Telecom and had been in the audience when I had made a presentation in Singapore about twelve years before. I did not recognise him, but I *was* in Singapore at that time and *did* make a presentation to Telecom. When I boarded the aircraft he was seated one place away from me.

In Lahore, I made some visits with the local agent and he took me to a traditional restaurant for lunch. There was a cholera epidemic in Pakistan at the time but my host assured me that we were going to a very good restaurant. He told me over lunch that it was dangerous to eat at market stalls and that mangoes could also cause gastric problems. Many Pakistan born, UK based, visiting friends and relatives had experienced problems after eating mangoes. This was a little alarming as a bowl of fruit had been placed in my room at the hotel and I had eaten a couple of mangoes the previous evening. I was assured that fruit bought by good hotels was probably all right.

The restaurant had a hot buffet area which was decorated like a traditional Pakistani village. Bread and various specialities were cooked to order over charcoal fires and there were a number of labelled dishes simmering on hotplates. One of these was 'sheep's legs' which I was urged to try on my second go around. I felt obliged to do so and spent some time fishing around in the pot to try and find some meat, with little success. I arrived back at our table with a plate full of bones with little meat on them. This amused my host greatly, as the dish was in fact the liquid in which the bones had been stewed for many hours. This is eaten with spoon and bread, and is very fatty.

Over lunch my host told me that he had undergone a triple heart bypass a year before, and he was only thirty-five. Sheep's legs was one of his favourite dishes, so perhaps it was not so surprising.

Baghdad Melon

In the early 1980s I spent a lot of time in Baghdad. In the summer months the temperature reaches fifty-five degrees centigrade and moving from an air-conditioned hotel outside into the shade is a physical shock. Moving into the sun from the shade is a further shock on the same scale.

In 1982 a number of first class hotels were completed in Baghdad. In addition, because of the war against Iran and the declining oil prices, there were less people travelling to Iraq on business and hotel rooms were easy to get. New automatic telephone and telex systems had also been installed and it was possible to communicate with ease in both directions. I usually stayed in the Meridian Hotel, which was on the bank of the Tigris on Sadoun Street and was one of the best run hotels that I have ever stayed in. The food was superb and typically French. There was an excellent swimming pool and the hotel was very well-managed. The staff were a mixture of nationalities; from Egypt, Pakistan, India, Mauritius, the Seychelles and many other countries. They were all friendly, but not cheeky or always looking for tips. They seemed to be well-motivated and efficient, but the supervision was not obvious. I always think of this as the best example of good management that I have experienced. I have also stayed in the Meridian in Cairo on the banks of the Nile, which is equally as good.

Some German companies had been commissioned to build breweries in Iraq and the beer, both draught and bottled, although not always available, was very good. The draught beer was served in half litres, which suited me very well, and it was possible to get seventy centilitre bottles of beer in many restaurants. I like to drink beer and felt obliged to prevent myself becoming dehydrated, even in the cooler weather. There are a number of primitive beer bars along Sadoun Street. These have leaning-height counters along the middle and sides of the room, a few stools and not much else. In the hot weather you are served with two half litres of beer together, without even ordering. The first goes down with barely a gulp and lays the dust, and the second is enjoyed more slowly. What a wonderful idea!

There are also many similarly primitive snack bars serving *döner* kebab and salad in pita bread envelopes. A colleague assured me that he often ate on the run at these establishments and the food was indeed very tasty, extremely inexpensive, and caused me no gastric problems. I also drank the tap water all the time I was there, with only minor problems, which could have been due to the amount of beer I was drinking.

Each hotel room had a small fridge in it. I was tipped off by a colleague that melons could be bought very cheaply nearby and that these, when kept in the fridge, made very good refreshment when returning from a day out in the heat. These were the large, dark green skinned melons with purple flesh and dozens of black seeds. I had eaten these in Cyprus many years before but had been told since, by someone who had lived in Cyprus, that some farmers increased the size of the fruit by injecting water into them. There had been cases of people getting food poisoning from eating melon, which had been attributed to polluted water having been used. In spite of this, and the fact that they had never been my favourite type of melon, I invested in one and placed it in the fridge.

We always spent a lot of time in taxis without air-conditioning, most of which had clear plastic coverings on the seats. The experience of sitting on these nicely warmed up sheets of plastic in the oppressive heat for up to an hour in heavy traffic can be imagined. On return to the hotel after a hot, dusty and often futile visit to a potential customer, the first actions would be to strip off the literally dripping clothes and cut a slice of melon. Biting into the cool, sweet and tremendously juicy fruit still counts as one of the most ecstatic gastronomic experiences of my life.

Dolcelatte

During lunch in Rome with the Italian branch manager of the company that I worked for, I ordered some Dolcelatte cheese. The waiter said that he had never heard of it. So too did my colleague, who asked me to write it down. This I did, but they still had not heard of it (I checked the spelling later and it was correct). I was sure that I had bought Dolcelatte in northern Italy on skiing holidays and in the local supermarket in Ascot and in Munich. My colleague was a mountain climber and skier and a frequent visitor to northern Italy, so it didn't seem to be a regional problem. But they were adamant and I began to doubt myself.

On a visit to northern Italy some years later, I stayed in an hotel in Varese near Lago Maggiore. I had dinner in the hotel restaurant and got chatting to the head waiter, who spoke good English. He had spent some years in England working in the Café Royal and in hotels in Guildford and Bristol. He was from Sardinia, but his wife was from northern Italy and was a member of the Berni family. He said that most of the Italian restaurateurs in England come from northern Italy. So too does a lot of the well-known Italian food such as Parma ham, and Parmesan and Gorgonzola cheese.

I took the opportunity to ask him about Dolcelatte, and he explained that it was the export name for a mild form of Gorgonzola, which is the name of the village where the famous cheese originated. Dolcelatte in fact means 'sweet milk' and is much more pleasant to the English ear than 'Gorgonzola', which always had the reputation when I was young of being a smelly, maggoty cheese.

He proved his point by asking a young waiter, who was studying English, which cheese on the trolley was the Dolcelatte and he replied "The Gorgonzola."

This made good sense as an international marketing ploy. The name Gorgonzola doesn't have a bad ring to it to Italians, so it doesn't need to be disguised. I wonder if we would be prepared to do the same for Stilton, which I have long believed has under-exploited export potential.

Lebanese Liver

I first visited Lebanon in the summer of 1969, as soon as I was qualified for a ten per cent air fare with BOAC. Lebanon was being promoted as an emerging holiday venue, where holiday-makers could swim in the Mediterranean in the morning and ski in the mountains in the afternoon.

At that time there were restrictions on the amount of currency that could be taken out of the UK, and traveller's cheques were entered in the back of the passport when purchased. I had arranged to meet the owner of the Beirut hotel in which I would be staying in London before the holiday, to pay part of the hotel costs, so that I would have more spending money in Lebanon. This I did with some concern as, of course, no receipt or written recognition of the payment was given. It turned out not to be a problem.

We met a number of Lebanese students at a beach club near the hotel early in the holiday. They were very friendly and hospitable, and invited us to go into the mountains with them for a *mezze*. *Mezzes* are eaten all through the Middle East and eastern Mediterranean, and consist of a number of common dishes of salad and meats from which everyone helps themselves.

Many of the richer people in Beirut have houses in the mountains east of the capital. They spend most of their time there in the summer, when it is very hot in the city below. We hitch-hiked up into the mountains with the students to a restaurant where we sat outside, with a magnificent view of Beirut and the Mediterranean.

The Lebanese, like most Arab nations, eat a lot of lamb. Our hosts told us with some glee that they ate 'all parts of the animal'. We were a little apprehensive about this and expected an eyeball or two. These did not appear, but it soon became apparent that some parts of the animal were eaten raw.

One local speciality is called *kibbeh*, which is raw, minced lamb mixed with herbs and cracked corn. Another consisted of cubes of raw lamb which had been marinated for some time in a mixture of herbs and oil. The third was raw lamb's liver.

Alcoholic drinks were readily available and the local beer and wine were very good. Also available was *arak* which is an aniseed based drink similar to Pernod and ouzo, and fairly strong. The meal was very enjoyable and high-spirited, with plenty of beer and *arak* drunk. I used to prefer my meat lightly cooked then, and sampled the *kibbeh* and marinated lamb without too much persuasion. I found them very pleasant. Towards the end of the meal I had drunk enough *arak* to be persuaded to eat some of the raw liver against my earlier, more sober, better judgement. Ever since then, whenever I have thought about that meal and the raw liver, I have shuddered.

My next visit to Lebanon was in 1995 after eighteen years of civil war, during which the centre of Beirut and the western, coastal part of the city had been virtually destroyed. On the telephone before the trip, I had told my agent of my previous stay, and that I had visited Baalbeck, a magnificent Roman temple in the Beqa'a Valley. This delighted him, and he said that he would take me there again when I visited. I immediately wished that I had kept my mouth shut about this, as the current Foreign Office advice then was not to travel out into the country. The Beqa'a Valley is where some of the British hostages were imprisoned for a while and where the Syrian-operated, Russian-built SAM missiles were stationed.

Most of the visit was spent in Beirut and the first time I got into my agent's Landcruiser, I stepped on a loaded AK47 assault rifle lying on the floor of the passenger side. I showed surprise at this, and he said that he had needed to go to the bank that morning. He did not say whether he was putting money in or withdrawing it without the normal formalities. He also kept a loaded handgun under his seat in the vehicle and another automatic weapon behind his filing cabinet in the office.

For my final meal, my host took me into the mountains to what he said was the best restaurant in Lebanon. It was very much grander and many times more expensive than the lively, but fairly simple restaurant that we had visited with the students those many years before. Predictably, a *mezze* was ordered and I recognised some familiar dishes. I eat my meat less rare than I did twenty-five years ago, but did manage some *kibbeh* and a cube or two of the raw, marinated mutton. I did have a couple of glasses of *arak*, but not enough to eat the raw liver, in spite of the gusto with which my fellow diners tucked in to it.

Portuguese Sardines

In the late 1960s and early 70s, when I was still a bachelor, I worked for BOAC. A major perk of working for an airline is that employees can get stand-by air tickets at vastly reduced fares. There were also 'Interline' travel packages, advertised at ridiculously low prices. These were aimed at travel agents, to give them experience of various overseas destinations and to fill aircraft seats during low season.

For reasons that I cannot now recall, I managed to get tickets on a four day package to Portugal. This consisted of two days in a fairly new hotel at Cascais, north of Lisbon, and two days in an old hotel in the centre of Lisbon.

At Cascais there is a famous casino and the Portuguese Grand Prix circuit. The main memory from this part of the trip is having my watch removed by a magician/pickpocket during a cabaret in the casino. I felt it being removed, although it was done very slickly, one handed, but he had gone on to the next victim before I could react. I have wondered many times since whether watches can really be removed without the subject knowing or if, like me, they do not get opportunity or feel it appropriate to protest.

The hotel in Lisbon was a lovely old, wood-panelled building. There were few guests but lots of staff in the restaurant, mostly being trained up to a reasonable standard before the start of the season. I studied the menu for something traditionally Portuguese and decided on sardines, which were described lyrically on the card, for a starter.

The style of service was very grand, with food being brought to the tables on trolleys under huge, domed, silver covers. A trolley was wheeled up to my table and, under the supervision of the head waiter, a young waiter removed the cover with something of a flourish. There, nestling in a bed of salad, was an opened tin of sardines. These were ceremoniously served from the tin onto my plate, the cover replaced, and the trolley wheeled away.

Wine Box in Kuwait

In 1992 and 1993 I spent a lot of time and effort in trying to sell electronic equipment to the Kuwait army as part of their re-equipping programme after the Iraqi invasion. I had found an agent who was an ex Kuwait army artillery man who seemed to have very good friends and contacts in the army.

He had stayed in Kuwait city in the early days after the invasion and later escaped by driving down into Saudi Arabia. He told tales of driving up to the border with Iraq in his Landcruiser and evacuating injured Kuwaitis from army bases which had been bombarded at the beginning of the Iraqi action. He had been stopped at gunpoint by Iraqi soldiers who were very suspicious of his mobile phone, which they thought was a military radio. He escaped by getting one of the soldiers to telephone his family in Basra on his mobile.

We drove out on the multi-lane, fast motorways toward the Iraqi border to visit an army base. As part of the Kuwaiti resistance efforts, all the road signs had been removed and were not yet replaced. We passed a huge area of desert near the hospital, where there were rows and rows of civil and military vehicles which had been destroyed in the massacre of the Iraqi troops by the allied forces as they fled from Kuwait. The area rapidly becomes featureless desert, and at one point my agent said that he was lost. A couple of British people had recently been captured and imprisoned by the Iraqis for straying over the ill-defined border between the countries, so this did not make me feel comfortable. However, we eventually found the army base before reaching the border and managed to conduct our business although, not unusually, the man with whom we had the appointment was not there.

On the return journey, my agent told me that he had no trouble getting alcohol and had regular parties at home with all types of alcoholic drinks. He asked what I normally drank at home, and I replied that I drank beer in the pub and wine at home. I thought that he was intending to invite me to one of his parties and was making sure that he had what I drank available, but he then said that some would be delivered to my hotel room that afternoon.

I realised later that I had unwittingly specified the most difficult alcoholic drinks to acquire, as they have a high weight to value ratio. Spirits are much more profitable to smuggle due to their higher value and lower bulk.

He telephoned me later at my hotel and said that his driver would be over in ten minutes with the drink, asking me to meet him in the hotel lobby. This I did, expecting the driver to arrive with a plain package which he would give me clandestinely, probably behind closed doors in my hotel room. In fact, he arrived with a Waitrose carrier bag containing a three litre wine box and a six-pack of lager which he handed over quite openly in the foyer. I took this quickly back to my room and kept it locked in my suitcase whenever I was out.

I rationed the booze for the few days I was there, drinking a beer before dinner and a couple of glasses of wine after. Just to be careful, I crushed the cans and dropped them surreptitiously in waste bins outside other people's rooms.

Mao Tai

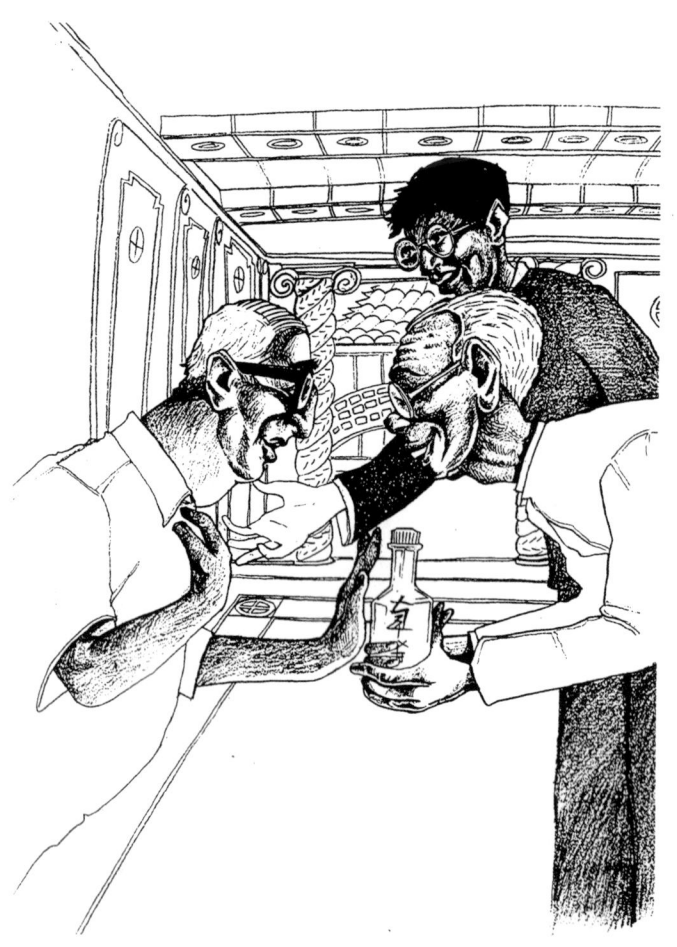

In January 1984 I made a trip to China via Hong Kong, where I met two American colleagues. One of these was an ex-army colonel who had originally been hired by the company to liaise with the US State Department, to hasten the granting of export licences for the militarily sensitive equipment that the company manufactured. A series of firings and resignations at the east coast division had left the Sales Manager's job vacant, and Jim Czapiewski had got it about a year earlier. Few people could pronounce his name and even fewer could spell it, and he was generally known as Jim C. He had a squat, burly physique with almost no neck, topped by a square head. He was about forty-five years of age, with a grizzled face and thick-lensed glasses. His reputation was for superficial, bustling energy and jet-setting around the world at a moment's notice.

When we arrived in Beijing we were met by two young-looking Chinese men, accompanied by a pretty Chinese girl. One of the men, Lu Ligang, was the very pleasant and bright interpreter of a Chinese party that I had met a couple of months before in the USA. He was married with a son of nearly a hundred days, which is a significant and highly celebrated age in a Chinese child's life.

Our luggage was loaded into two elderly cars and we were taken to the Beijing Hotel which overlooks the Forbidden City and Tianenmen Square. (A number of foreign journalists sheltered in this hotel when fleeing the troops during the massacre in the square in 1989.) As we were waiting to check in, Joe C invited the Chinese party to have dinner with us. The hotel had a number of dining rooms and Lu Ligang asked where we wanted to eat. Joe C said, "Let's have a Mongolian pot." Although this normally had to be ordered in advance, Lu Ligang managed to arrange it.

The meal is a Mongolian version of a fondue, and was a memorable experience and a wonderful introduction to Beijing. The 'pot' was a cauldron of very tasty soup which was set in the middle of the table on a heater which kept it simmering. Around it was a turntable with a number of plates with meat, vegetables and bread on them. The technique was the same as a fondue. Pieces of food were speared on long-handled forks and then poached in the pot. It was a highly enjoyable meal, with much toasting of Lu Ligang's son and general merriment in hunting for lost food in the pot.

We had a number of meetings over the next few days and, during one, Joe C had ostentatiously invited about sixteen customer and trading company personnel to a banquet in a private dining room in the hotel. This was a traditional part of the business process, and twenty people is a good number to get a varied mixture of dishes. Joe had specified the menu and we had shark's fin soup to start. One of my other colleagues, who had lived in China for many years, told me that it was top quality and must have cost a fortune. A team of people would have been up all night, stripping the meat from the fin and shredding it. There were a lot of speeches, with Joe heading the proceedings from our side. Many toasts were drunk, using a fiery liquid called *Mao Tai*. It transpired that there are two types of toasts. One is 'quing', which means 'please' and when toasted thus the *Mao Tai* can be sipped. (A Hong Kong born friend of mine told me that the Italian toast of 'chin chin' is derived from 'quing'.) The other is 'gambay' which means 'empty glass' or 'bottoms up', and not to observe it is to lose face. Lu Ligang told me later that his colleagues had decided to get Joe C drunk and had taken it in turns to 'gambay' him. Joe's character would not allow him to refuse the challenge, and at the end of the two and a half hour meal he was very drunk. As we went to the cashier's office to pay the bill, the Director of the trading company, who was the leader of the Chinese delegation, brought the bottle of *Mao Tai* and ceremonially presented it to Joe, who 'obviously enjoyed it so much'. Joe never wanted to see a drop of *Mao Tai* again in his life at that stage and handed the bottle over to me. (I still have the remnants of this at home and it has not improved with age. Even a sniff of the contents is enough to encourage guests who have outstayed their welcome to go home.) He then stumbled off to bed, telling me to settle the bill. "No chance," said I, and made sure that the cashier's office knew the banquet had been organised by Joe.

That evening, we were obliged to attend another banquet at a restaurant some distance from the hotel with representatives of another trading company. This was not until eight o'clock and Joe had resurfaced by then, but was less than his usual ebullient self. The meal took the usual two and a half hours and it was bitterly cold in the restaurant. None of us felt like eating much, and the waitress was dressed in a filthy white coat. The food was not very good. We had a large fish on the bone which did not seem very fresh and tasted muddy. We all ate a respectable amount, whilst casting sideways glances at the waitress and wondering whether the standards in the kitchen were better than those in the laundry. We finished with a memorable sweet called 'dragon's beard' which was a nest of very fine, sweet, crisp noodles that melted in the mouth. We all slept well that night.

My American colleagues finished their discussions and headed back to the USA. I stayed on to conclude my negotiations and sign a contract. When I went to check out, I discovered that Joe C *had* left without paying the bill for the banquet and had told the cashier that I would settle up. I was furious, especially after the lordly way that he had hosted the banquet, but I had no alternative but to pay up gracefully. I bumped into Joe a couple of years later at a hotel in Brighton, after I had left the company. I told him that he still owed me for the banquet and he said, 'Well you got the business'. The company I then worked for had arranged a dinner at Arundel Castle that evening for about a hundred people and I had visions of inviting Joe along and sticking him with the bill, but I didn't. I will get him one day.

Kassler Rippe

I lived in Munich from 1980 to the end of 1983. Soon after my family arrived we visited Ravensberg, where we had lunch. I had studied German for some years, but was to find out when working in the language that it needed a lot of improvement. We studied the menu and ordered *Kassler Rippe*, mainly for the accompanying vegetables, which were pureed potato and sauerkraut, suitable for our six month old son. We were very impressed by the attitude of German restaurants and pubs, where children were made welcome. When requested, extra plates would be willingly provided on which the kids could be given a portion of their parent's meal.

The *Kassler Rippe* turned out to be a rack of smoked pork chops and was delicious and I urged my wife to try and buy it from the local butcher. We did not make any effort to translate, but had looked up 'chop' for which we had found the translation of *Kotelett*. My wife, who spoke less German than I did, made several attempts to buy *Rippe Koteletten* without success. I told my German colleagues about this and they found it very amusing. *Rippe* means 'rib', so my wife had been asking for rib chops. *Kassler* describes the smoked rack which we enjoyed many times after we had found out how to order it.

During my first days in Munich, before my family arrived, I lived opposite the Hofbräu brewery. As a keen beer drinker in the beer drinking capital of the world, this was very acceptable. I often ate in the beer garden attached to the brewery and regularly took visitors to the famous *Hofbräuhaus* in the middle of the city.

On a visit to Abu Dhabi in the early 90s, I stayed in a magnificent hotel right on the beach. The United Arab Emirates is one of the more liberal Arab states and it is possible to buy alcohol there without any problems. There was a German-style Bierstube in the hotel where I had an evening meal. The speciality of the day was *Kassler Rippe* and the beer on sale was Hofbräu, served in one litre glasses. I ordered both and the meal brought back many good memories of Munich. But, I mused, not without a slight feeling of guilt, eating pork, washed down with a litre or two of beer, must be the height of decadence in a Muslim state.

Ethiopian Banquet

My first visit to Ethiopia was via Turkey, where I had arranged to carry out demonstrations of some electronic equipment that I had taken with me. This took place in Istanbul, and involved a lot of carrying of the fairly heavy equipment. In addition, when I go on a long trip I have to take a lot of technical data, and my case was very heavy.

About two weeks before the trip I had developed some pain in my right shoulder, which had been stiff for about five years. Within half a day this had developed into acute discomfort and I could barely move it. I made a rare visit to the doctor, who prescribed me some anti-inflammatory tablets. These were supposed to be taken after a main meal, due to the adverse effect they could have on digestion. I took a tablet at about six o'clock in the evening and the effect was dramatic. By eight o'clock, I could move my shoulder freely and after the second tablet the next day, my shoulder was freer than it had been since the stiffness had first developed.

I consulted the doctor as to whether I should complete the course of tablets (I had only taken half of one of the two packs supplied), and he said that I only needed to take them when required. So, against the advice of my wife, I took only the other half of the packet that I had started, about five tablets, on my trip.

On my last day in Istanbul my shoulder became painful again, probably due to the carrying of heavy equipment and luggage. This did not disturb me too much as I thought that one or two tablets would sort out the problem, as they did the previous time. My flight to Addis Ababa was via Dubai and, as I had spent a weekend in Istanbul recently and the hotel swimming pool was closed, I changed my flight to stay in Dubai for the weekend. I had stayed in a very nice hotel near the airport a few months before and managed to get a room there as it was summer, very hot, and there were not many guests. My shoulder seemed to be improving and I did some swimming, which seemed to have an adverse effect. By the time I reached Addis Ababa I had run out of tablets and my shoulder was still uncomfortable.

Meetings with customers were fairly informal and the main meeting of my visit took place in my agent's twenty year old car, on the way out to a military workshop just outside the city. When I got into the front passenger seat, Michael was already sitting in the back seat. I was introduced to him and when I leaned over the back to shake his hand, the pain in my shoulder was agonising. This was worsened by the journey to the workshop over deeply rutted tracks in the old, stiff suspensioned car. The Ethiopian people are very warm and friendly and give double-handed, long and strong handshakes, each of which exacerbated the pain in my shoulder. There was no chance of obtaining more anti-inflammatory tablets in Ethiopia so I dosed myself with pain-killers and hoped that it would improve.

It had not by the time my agent took me, with his wife, to an ethnic Ethiopian restaurant. The restaurant was circular around a central raised part where we had coffee after the meal. There were low tables and backless chairs round the room and, in the middle of each place, a one metre high, sixty centimetre diameter, cloth covered cylinder with a pointed top. My host informed me that we would eat with our fingers and I established, with some dismay, that it was custom to use only the right hand.

After our order had been taken, two waiters approached our table with what looked like a large pewter teapot. This turned out to contain water to wash our hands before the meal. My host's wife and I made a token effort at rinsing our hands but he did a full job, with soap and much rubbing, wringing and rinsing of his hands. As we were doing this, another waiter appeared with a large platter covered in what looked like spongy towels, which I anticipated were for drying our hands. They were not, and we had to dry our hands on paper napkins although, strangely, we *were* brought towels when the ritual was repeated at the end of the meal.

The cloth was whisked away from the cylinder in front of us and a wicker Babycham-glass-shaped object with a conical top was revealed. The top was removed and the platter placed in the shallow bowl in the top of the pedestal. Then, the contents of various dishes were spooned in turn onto the towels, which turned out to be sheets of maize bread. The procedure then is to tear off a piece of bread, which is very soft and spongy, and use it to grasp portions of the spicy stew-like dishes. The whole package is then eaten. I was encouraged to try everything, which meant continually reaching across to the other side of the platter. I could only do this by supporting my right arm with my left, and the whole meal was very uncomfortable. The maize bread was very sweet and the meat, of which there was a lot, was very chewy so, although it was an interesting experience, it was not one of my most enjoyable meals.

In addition, there were some Ethiopian singers and dancers performing throughout the meal. The dances from one of the regions involved much very rapid shaking of the shoulders. The performers moved around the room and invited diners to join them in turn, which most did enthusiastically. My hosts encouraged me to take part when it was our turn, which caused my shoulder to tense up even more in anticipation. I was in such discomfort that I declined the invitation. In spite of my explanations of my problem, I felt that my fun loving, try anything reputation had suffered.

My next stop was South Africa, where I managed to buy some anti-inflammatory tablets at a local chemist's without a prescription. I now always travel with a plentiful supply of the tablets although, predictably, the problem has not recurred since then.

Indian Dogs

My first visit to India was to make some demonstrations of electronic equipment to a number of Defence customers. The initial stop was in Delhi where my agents had arranged a presentation to an audience of high-ranking officers from all three armed services.

The next venue was in Hyderabad, where the Indian aircraft and associated industries are based. The flight from Delhi was at around six o'clock in the morning, which meant getting up at about four o'clock and leaving the hotel at four thirty, before breakfast was served.

The presentation in Hyderabad was in a medium-sized conference room in the local office of the agent. The presentation began at ten o'clock with the room comfortably full. During the next half hour, more and more people arrived and the room became packed to capacity.

The weather was warm and the room was cooled by two elderly air-conditioners in windows at each end of the room, whose main contribution to the environment was the rattle of their very noisy fans. In the centre, near to my presentation position, was a voltage stabiliser which was humming loudly.

Educated Indians speak arguably the best and most complicated English in the world. However, some have very strong accents and it was difficult to understand some of the more complicated questions that were being asked from the back of the room in the high ambient noise level. Many questions were posed, and the most aggressive questioner was also the most difficult to understand. He became increasingly aggressive each time I asked him to repeat something and by midday I was ready for a drink and some food. A buffet lunch was provided which, because of the mixed religion audience, was vegetarian. It consisted of some dubious looking stews which I made only a token effort at eating.

The presentation went on in the afternoon and we left for the airport at around 4 p.m. By the time we had taken off and the meal service had begun at about six o'clock, I was starving. The flight attendants served the basic tray and then asked each passenger whether they wanted a 'veg or non-veg', hot main course. I opted for non-veg and received a warm, foil wrapped package. When I opened it, it contained what looked like two large, black, dog turds. I was so hungry that I ate them, whatever they were, but the initial shock of opening that parcel is still a vivid memory.